Heaven's Royalty, That's Me!

Selena Holston Gabriel

WestBow Press books may be ordered through booksellers or by contacting:

WestBow Press
A Division of Thomas Nelson & Zondervan
1663 Liberty Drive
Bloomington, IN 47403
www.westbowpress.com
1 (866) 928-1240

Illustration Credit: Stacy Bearden

Scripture quotations are from New Revised Standard Version Bible, copyright © 1989 National Council of the Churches of Christ in the United States of America. Used by permission. All rights reserved worldwide.

ISBN: 978-1-9736-6594-6 (sc)
ISBN: 978-1-9736-6595-3 (e)

Library of Congress Control Number: 2019907690

Print information available on the last page.

WestBow Press rev. date: 10/14/2019

Author's Dedication

For my daughter Micah, for girls all over the
globe, and to the one reading this book:
Dream big. Very big. Hold tightly to the dreams that God has for you. He
will match your gifts, strengths, and creative abilities to the needs of the
world and use you to make a compassionate difference. You are very loved.

It's so fun to play dress-up,
To wear a royal gown,
To enter a magical world
Of wands, jewelry and crowns.

It's so fun to play dress-up,
But I hope you know,
You're already a princess,
Here's how the story goes...

You're already a princess,
You don't have to pretend,
It's written in God's Word,
On that you can depend.

You're already a princess,
Daughter of Christ the King,
You have access to God's throne,
Part of His royal family.

You're already a princess,
You didn't earn this place,
You're an heir of God's Kingdom,
You're a gift of His grace.

You were made in His image,
Designed by His hands,
Called for His purpose,
His will, His plan.

Fearfully and
Wonderfully made.

Psalm 139:14

Created to make a difference,
Even before your birth,
To share all that is within you,
To be a blessing on earth.

Your skills and strengths
Reflect God above

Use them to serve your neighbor,

To demonstrate God's love.

Offer your gifts and talents,
Yet be discerning too,
Lead with kindness and compassion
In everything you do.

19

And when you fall down,
Or need to be loved,
Put your trust in Him,
By His strength you overcome.

21

Treasure God's word,
Hide it in your heart,
Don't compare yourself to others,
You've been set apart.

Live by the Fruit of the Spirit,
Love, joy and peace,
Exercise self-control,
And give generously.

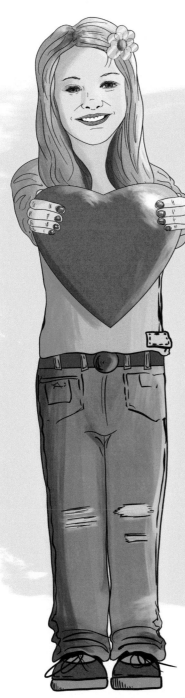

The fruit of the Spirit is love, joy, peace, patience, kindness, generosity, faithfulness, gentleness, and self-control.

Galatians 5:22-23

You don't need to be perfect,
Or ace every test,
You are loved and accepted
So just do your best!

You have infinite worth,
You're a priceless treasure,
Be confident in that,
Emboldened beyond measure.

The next time you play dress-up,
Remember dresses are fine,
But real beauty is on the inside,
So let your light shine!

31

You belong at the King's table,
The Majesty's tea,
You are His adopted child,
And that's not make-believe!

You belong at the King's table.

You will always have a seat.

You are His forever daughter.

A Princess. Heaven's Royalty!

Printed in the United States
By Bookmasters